Of Vines and Missions

Of Vines and Missions

By Alvin J. Gordon

Illustrations by Ted De Grazia

PUBLISHED BY NORTHLAND PRESS / FLAGSTAFF 1971

This book is dedicated
to growers and winemakers every-
    where – individuals, companies,
corporations – whether in Mexico or
    California or elsewhere, whether
on or off the mission route.

    Their spirit is high, their endeavors
honest, their product a delight
    to many.

                    Salud!

                    ALVIN GORDON

                    TED DE GRAZIA

*H*ERE
high above
the Valley of the Moon
I see the plants
the grape rootstock
feeding luxuriously
on the deep red
shale soil
and sucking the moisture
held long after
the winter rains
have passed
waiting to receive
the budding on
of Barbera
of Chenin Blanc
of Pinot Noir

I look down
upon the many
varieties
decorating the flat lands
with bouquets of green
in the moist
air of spring

3

the lush
clusters of fruit
green and
white and
deep purple
as autumn
turns the
leaves to
myriad
yellows and browns

How many times
this valley has
sustained me
through manifest trials
As "the Lord
is my shepherd . . .
He maketh me
to lie down in
green pastures"
so have I lain
between
the warm
breasts
of its
gentle hills
and recovered
the strength
the belief

5

the will
so have
I recovered
myself and myself
to the selves
around me

It has long been known
as the
Valley of the Moon
"Sonoma"
"Sonoma"
music
in the ancient
Indian name
and this
I know
as truth
this moon
in this valley
unlike
any moon
in the world
to me at least
or perhaps at most
carries
no mystery
projects

7

only warmth
that fires
a glow
the depressed heart
with confidence
in the permanence
of beauty
and love
love
of a lover
and the love
of a mother
sustaining

This
may be
why the grape
grows well
in the valley

For wine is
a woman
and woman
is a song
and a flower
and a love
So wine

9

like a woman
is a song
and a flower
and a love
And the valley
opens its arms
and its heart
to the vine
nurtures it
with moisture
and hot sun
and the warmth
of a benevolent moon
Sonoma
Sonoma
I hear the song
again and again

The first
Franciscan fathers
placed into
the waiting arms
of the earth
the first
plantings of the vines
the Mission grape
whose juices

made the
mellow sacramental
wine
staining with
its permanence
the chalices
of many beliefs
thousands of years over

Then time –
and man
aware of the
potential
came from the
world around
from Spain
from Austria
from Italy
from France
Came looking
for the new world
and found an old
a homeland
blessed with
the soil and moisture
and the sun
and the moon

13

And they planted
in Sonoma
some in the valley
some on the
sloping hillsides
the hardy
Zinfandel
Carignan
the more delicate
Cabernet
Pinot
Traminer
Chablis
Chenin Blanc
and depending
upon the soil
and the altitude
depending
upon the taste
of the individual
or individuals
these varieties
matured
and the whole valley
became pregnant
and gave birth

And love was
in the valley
as it is today
as the vines
spread out
from the lowlands
and move upward
perhaps seeking the beams
of the bright warm moon

I sit upon
a Sonoma hilltop
as the September moon
is slowly rising
drinking the sturdy
Carignan perhaps
a relative of
the Mission grape
and I look up
upon the tall
olive trees
their leaves
shimmering in the moonlight
trees planted
some hundred years ago
by those who
settled on this

17

height and brought
from Italy
the ancient symbols
of homesteading
olives for peace
for strength
the oil that
lighted the Hebrew candelabra
the oil of Catholic blessings
And they brought
cuttings and planted vines
and settled into
the new country
confident in the
security of the future
And they propagated

The moon is full
and round and warm
I hear the barking
of the foxes
I toast Sonoma !

Is wine
a missionary ?
Has it a place
in the milleniums

19

to return again
and again
to nurse
and nurture others?
Or does it feel
when spreading
its buds
in the confusion
of the early
spring rains
and sun
like the
omnipresent mother
satisfied
when it can
gladden the hearts
of birds and foxes and men?

I look out
over the rolling
hills at the
youthful sproutings
and see behind
them the gnarled
decayed and
rotted shells
of their unattended forebears
I toast the pioneers!

21

Suddenly
a figure arises
outlined against
the horizon
A gust of wind
blows out
his ample robes
and spreads them wide
His bare feet shine
his arms
outstretched
he seems to soar
with the power
of the great eagle
surveying the earth's potential

It is a fantasy
I know
It is an image of
the Franciscan Padres
Sonoma their most
northerly of missions
of olives
of grapes

23

But strongly
persists the fantasy
and I begin
to reminisce
From whence
came here the vine
and when?

The moon is brilliant
I let my glass
stand empty

Spain
a dominant power
Cortez
a dominant figure
followed by many others
seeking the treasures
of the Indies
found the silver
and the gold
and the fertility
of Mexico

25

The black robed Jesuits
moved out from
central Mexico
into the hinterland
linking the wilds
by a chain of missions
moving northward
converting the Indians
to Catholicism
settling them into
organized communities
and planting olive trees
and vines

I drink and think of
Masefield
"Stately Spanish galleon . . .
Dipping through the Tropics
by the palm-green shores . . .

Spanish galleons
carrying spices
and silks and other treasures
battled their way
between the Orient
and La Paz
Often losing time
ships and men

27

ARIZONA 1970

men dying from scurvy
The port of La Paz
on Baja California
offered fresh fruits of cactus
which was their only cure

Attempts were made in vain
to settle this natural harbor
The natives were hostile
controlled by the king
of the pearl divers
who feared the invasion
of his lucrative trade

But the urge for
territorial expansion
and the burning fire
of the Padres
kept alive the
desire for settlements

What were the natives
at this time ?
Various Indians
many shackled
by myriad superstitions
and claustrophobia

29

Their radius was
at the most thirty miles
their wants simple
They feared a wall
and lived in the open
The Wizard Gopher
was their controlling god
He dwelled
beneath the earth
and sucked down
to his dwelling
whatever he desired

Over much of the gulf
one god dominated
and demanded
all the fish
sacrificed to him
So in the face
of this abundance
the Indians
ate grasshoppers
and roots
and waited
for the Pitahaya cactus
to bear its sweet fruit

31

De Grazia
ARIZONA
1970

Here they convened
for the gourmand harvest
which sometimes
endured for several months
and they gorged themselves

I raise my glass
Salud !
Padre Kino !

In the September of 1683
the master missionary
Padre Kino
sailed from Sonora
on the mainland
confident of his mission
having accomplished wonders
with the Tarahumares
the Yaquis and the Mayos
on the mainland
the fusion
of the native belief
with severe Catholicism –
the Yaqui deer dancers
performing at the
entrance of the church
from dark till dawn

33

a huge fire lighting the scene
the incessant beat of the water drum
interrupted by the
tolling of the hours
by the melodious
mission bells

He sailed from the
crusted shoreline
He witnessed
the fish formations
in the clouds
as though jealous
of the inhabitants
of the sea below
one tiger shark
one killer whale
moved by the
high winds
chasing schools
of lesser fish
Then all
disappearing
into the red haze
of the sunset

35

DeGrazia
ARIZONA
1970

He saw the
giant Manta Ray
leap into the air
to shake off parasites
that irritate its
sunbath
Then suspended
for a moment
falling flat and hard
shaking the sea's surface
and causing waves
that travel far
and join others
in their adventures
And after the
sun had set
on starless nights
there was nothing
Even the water
upon which the
bark was floating
became an unknown entity
only its occasional swell
the reminder of existence
and faithful buoyancy

And on the morning
of the seventh day

37

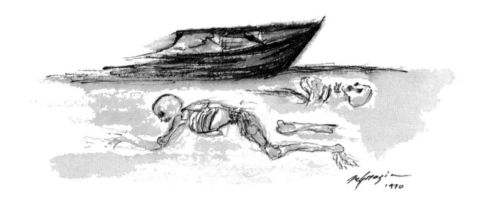

his powerful eyes
scanned the shoreline
of his destination
tried to discern
between the dry
desolate islands
some with inviting beaches
to seduce a man
then parch him
until his bones
dry up to dust
and blow away
And the mainland
with its chalky
forbidding mountains
dotted only here
and there with greenery

Was he aware
of the turbulence
that oceans
wrack upon the land
even when the
seemingly placid tides
run their watery fingers
up onto a shore
carrying rocks and shells

wearing down
the roughness
of their exteriors
until all is sand?
Was he aware that
sometimes the tides
chased by the violence
of hurricanes
create
new and lovely beaches
of peace and solitude
but ever ever
threaten with
destruction?

Kino fired with
adventure
set foot upon
the barren shore
of central Baja California
The necessities
for survival and
establishment of a
colony were unloaded
and the ship
returned to the mainland
for more supplies

Water was scarce
but Kino's
hope prevailed
He taught the
Indians to make
adobes and
began construction
of a church
A month later
the ship returned
with supplies from
the Yaqui missions
and fruit trees
and grape vines

With zealous joy
Kino and his
few converts
went to work
creating ingenious methods
to bring religious understanding
to the natives
He would catch a fly
and dip it into water
until it was
apparently dead
Then
he would place
it in the sun

43

and when its wings
became dry
it would fly away
The inquisitive eyes
of the Indians
witnessed
a resurrection

Two years they tried
but all in vain
Many of the Indians
had become converts
but the drought
continuing for those years
moved them from
the beginnings of
a mission settlement
back to the
ways of the nomad
to search out
their food
The master missionary
was forced to give up
and his precious vines
were abandoned
to the severity
of nature

45

He was the last
to board the ship
and sadly watch as
his footprint in
the sand was slowly
washed away
by the gentle tides

I let my empty glass stand
Again I see the apparition
on the horizon

Immediately he planned another trip
this time with Salvatierra
Five months passed
Kino was needed on the mainland
to move the settlements northward

I fill my glass and drink
Salud !
Padre Salvatierra !

In October Salvatierra
of light Italian spirit

47

landed at Baja California
carrying a magnificent
image of the
Virgin of Loreto
Stoutly he held up
a giant cross
as the Indians
remembering Kino's teachings
kneeled and kissed it

Southward he led his
little band until
they reached an oasis
The cross was erected
and our Lady of Loreto
the image of the Virgin
whose dwelling had
miraculously moved
from Nazareth
to the shores of
the Adriatic sea
was carried in procession
and carefully placed
upon a pedestal
as the boom
of cannons
shattered the holy silence

49

The early missionary Padres
carrying with them
the olive branch of peace
and cuttings from
the Mission vine
their feet first shod with boots
of Spanish make
or moulded by
newly trained
Indian hands
With time in
the remote areas
as these boots disintegrated
crude sandals
were devised
Then sometimes
barefoot
they left their imprints
in the coastal mud
the desert sands
even as if carved
into the rock of ages

Feet
The feet that tromped
the mud to form adobes
for the structure
of the House of Worship

51

The feet that danced
upon the newly tanned hides
to wear away their stiffness
The toes that tucked
the earth around
the newly planted vine
The feet that stomped
the grapes to make
the gentle Mission wine
the powerful aguardiente

Then the feet that bore
the weight of the giant crosses
south to San Jose del Cabo
north to Santa Maria
into the forbidding mountains
San Ignacio, Guadalupe
Black Robes moving over Baja

And then by political rule
the Black Robes depart
abandon their great works
their missions
their orchards
their olives
and their vines

53

It is said
that when the
Franciscans first trod
upon the soil of Baja
the ghost of
a Jesuit Padre
appeared before
their procession
and prophesied
that in the year of 1812
their future missions
would be doomed

Then what with the vines ?

I drink heartily and
I become the vine

I am the vine
of the missions
abandoned for a time
and yet my strength
gave me my survival
until I was old
and dry and gnarled

55

beaten by the
sun and wind
and salt was in my veins
But I was alive

Then came my
restorers in robes of brown
the ardent Serra
carefully selecting
the young off-shoots
that I had sent out every year
hoping for the procreation
And they planted these
and they grew hardy
as impervious to disease
and drought as I

And so my tribe reborn
increased
In oases by the seashore
in pockets and crevasses
in the mountains
Now they take
the fruit my children bear
expose them tranquilly to
the burning sun
until their sugar sweetness rises
their tough skins soften

57

Then deft and gentle fingers
take the blackest of the berries
for the making of the wine
and the others are fermented
and distilled into the
aguardiente brandy
And again I make the wines
of masses and communions
and to lift the soul of man
and the aguardiente brandy
to raise his spirits
from the doldrums of
his barren isolated day

Salud !
Padre Serra !

1769
News of the settling
of the Russians
and the British
in Alta California
reaches the
imperialistic ears
of Spain
They must push northward

Again the feet
of missionaries
and soldiers
and horses
and cattle
with provisions
and tools
and olives
and vines
driven by the imperialist
and led by the
ardor of religion
moving slowly slowly northward
until the bay of San Diego
Here the cross
the olive
the vine
is planted
and Alta California
becomes a part of Spain

And the vine
moved with the
ardent Serra
to Monterey
There in a verdant valley
nestled in the rolling hills

61

of central California
the mission
San Antonio de Padua
was founded
and the Mission
vine planted
Then at San Luis Obispo
another link
in Serra's dream
his Rosary of Missions
Next San Juan Capistrano
where the knowing swallows
return each year
on the same date
to nest in the eaves
and the belfry
Then San Buenaventura
Although it was his last
his disciples had brought
the total up to nine
and the work continued
The Monterey mission
found the land
unfertile
The vine did not flourish
Serra moved it
to Carmel and

the vines were
planted in the Carmel Valley
and the mission San Carlos
Borromeo de Carmelo
prospered

It was here
that Serra exercised
his duties as
father-president
of all the California missions
and it was here
in August of 1784
never satisfied
with his accomplishments
but ever pleased
with the beauty
and bounteousness
of his surroundings
he died

He would not know
that the Jesuit ghost's
prediction would
come to pass
that earthquakes in 1812

65

would topple the belfrys
and shatter the
adobe walls
of many of his efforts
Nor did he
live to witness
the heartbreaking
secularization
of 1836 to 1838
the end for many years of his
Rosary of Missions

Here I sit
overlooking
the Sonoma Valley in full moonlight
the home of
the last of the missions
San Francisco Solano
founded in 1823
in the heart
of the wine country
and I imagine myself
living in a thriving
mission community

The gentle call
to awakening
of the sweet
mission bells
as the sun's
first timid rays
creep into the valley
The shock
of the chill
as I fling off
my serape
and touch
my bare feet
to the damp cold
tiles of the floor
and search
out my sandals
in the half-dark
of my tiny room
The heavy wool
of my brown robes
begins to warm
my skin
and I join
the hushed shuffle
of sandaled feet
across the courtyard
through the arched arcade

and into the
House of God
where the golden
altar candles
seem to radiate heat
to the body
and to the soul

As I exit
I turn toward the
pat pat pat
of the women
making the tortillas
while others are
hunched over
the limestones
grinding the corn
into meal
Nearby the kitchen
is busy
preparing beans
dried beef
hot sauces
and pozole
and thin corn gruel
delicately seasoned
with sugar and cinnamon

a favorite of the Indians
and the Padres
and the small
contingent of military
The refectory is
humming with discussion
A visiting traveller
bears the news
of faraway places
Plans are made
for the day's work

I stroll through
adjacent buildings
Hides have been
scraped clean
the tallow used
for candlemaking
the hides then tanned
and rolled
The bare feet
of the Indians
dance upon the roll
to make the
leather pliable
for saddles and belts
for boots and sandals

73

I hear the
clanging of
the ironsmiths
forming nails and plows
lanterns and gates
bands for the wheels of
the awkward oxcarts
and delicate horse carriages

I hear the creaking
of the heavy log
the heaving of the mule
as blindfolded he
pushes forward
more and more
in his circle
of destiny
And the hand-hewn
stone wheel
through which
the great log passes
squashes olives with
its ponderous weight
as the lowly
beast of burden

75

shares in the making
of the hallowed
oil of the olive

I see the Indians
bringing basket after basket
piled high with grapes
and unloading them
into huge adobe
bins plastered smooth with lime
where others
press with their feet
to crush the grapes
The juices flow into
fermenting vats
in the cellar below

My morning has been full
The odors of
the fat falling
from a spitted beef
onto the hot coals
whet my appetite
and I welcome the
call to dinner

77

A glass of aguardiente
a tumbler of mission wine
and then a short siesta

I visit the fields
observing the ingenious
irrigation systems
the rudiments
of animal husbandry
Traders from
the Spanish galleons
moving from mission
to mission –
each established
one day's ride
from one another –
arrive laden
with cloths and spices
and sugar and chocolate
They trade with the Padres
for tallow and hides
and aguardiente

The odor of
hot chocolate brewing
leads me toward

the refectory
for the light supper
Then the bells announce
the vesper service
The clear Indian voices
of the choir
sing with religious fervor
in well enunciated Latin
which they do not understand
The joy in their voices
predominates

Back on my Sonoma hilltop
I pour another
glass of wine
The moon is waning

1836
The secularization
of these glorious missions
their subsequent
disintegration
The Mission grape
persisted along
with the mystery
surrounding its variety

81

I feel that the hearty
Carignan which
I have been drinking
stems from
the Padres' endeavors
I look upwards
and see in the
faltering moonlight
my young vines
Traminer
Chenin Blanc
Pinot Noir
Barbera
I wonder whether
most of the rootstock
is of the Mission family
The image of the Padre
on my hill
has disappeared
The fog rising from the valley
leaves me shrouded in
solitude

I drink another
full glass
Salud !
Padres and pioneers !

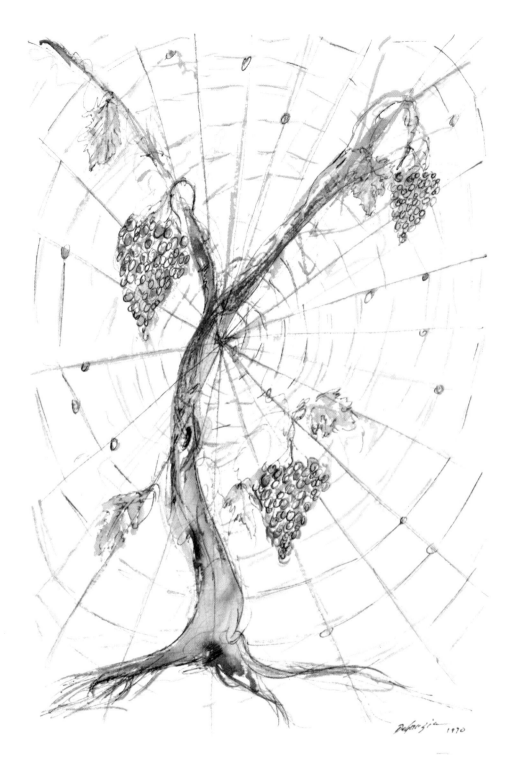

Around many of their missions
old vines still grow
perhaps the Mission grape
still used
in Catholic ceremony
perennial memorial
to the great settlers
of the past

Had I been nursed
on burro's milk
and weaned
on dried beef
of the bull
which was and
in some places
still is the symbol
of the strength
of the man
would I have been
able to trod
the uncharted
paths of the Padres ?
Would not then a
glass of wine be
needed to mellow
the machoism

the over-masculine
tendency of one
so fed and then
devoted to the
celibate life ?
My feelings now
are strong and positive
but mellowed by
the wondrous
well-aged wine

And as in
religion
from the revelries
of Bacchus
to the orthodoxy
of Judaism
Catholicism
and many others
so stands
the wine
significant to man
a mellowing
blending of
himself into
the world around him

Wine
whether it owes
its existence
to European forebears
or the rich valleys
of southern and
central California
the rolling hills
of Santa Clara
Livermore and Lodi
of Mendocino
Napa and Sonoma

Wine is a woman
and woman
is a song
and a flower
and a love
So wine like a woman
is a song
and a flower
and a love

A cup of love
A cup of love
from Sonoma
From the valley of Sonoma
a cup of love !

Bibliography

Prescott, William — *Conquest of Mexico* — Harper Brothers

Diaz del Castillo, Bernard — *Discovery and Conquest of Mexico* — Farrar Straus

Lasuen, Fermin Francisco de — *Writings* — The Academy of American Franciscan History

Catholic Encyclopedia

Lewis, Oscar — *Here Lived the Californians* — Rhinehart

Lewis, Oscar — *California Heritage* — Crowell

Atherton, Gertrude — *California: An Intimate History* — Liveright

Cleland, Robert Glass — *From Wilderness to Empire* — Knopf

Hanna, Phil Townsend — *California Through Four Centuries* — Farrar & Rhinehart

Dunne, Peter Masten — *Black Robes in Lower California* — University of California Press

Bolton, Herbert Eugene — *Rim of Christendom* — H. E. Russel

Hobart, Alice Tesdale — *The Cup and the Sword* — Bobbs

Berger, John A. — *The Franciscan Missions of California* — Doubleday

Hawthorne, Hildegarde — *California Missions* — Suydom

The California Missions — Lane

Blanco, Antonio de Fierro — *The Journey of the Flame* — Houghton

Leggett, Herbert — *Early History of Wine Production in California* — Wine Institute

Melville, John — *Guide to California Wines* — Nourse

Stevenson, Robert Louis — *Silverado Squatters* — Scribner

Wine Handbook Series, Book I — Wine Advisory Board

Haraszthy, Augustin — *Report on the Grapes and Wines of California*

Reene, Lloyd and Alice — *Gift of the Grape* — Filmer Bros.

Schoonmaker, Frank — *Encyclopedia of Wines* — Hastings House

Beck, Fred — *The Fred Beck Wine Book* — Hill and Wong

California Wine Country — Sunset

Terry's Guide to Mexico — Doubleday

Gulick — *Lower California Guidebook* — Arthur Clark

Fielding's Travel Guide to Europe — William Sloane

Spain — *Holiday Magazine Travel Guide*

Teide — *Diccionario de Vinos Españoles*

Vignoble et Vins D'Alsace — Colmar, France

Veronelli, Luigi— *I vini d'Italia*

Jacquelin and Poulen — *The Wine and Vineyards of France* — Paul Hamlyn

Aguado, Afrodisio — *España Turistica*

Michelin — France

I am grateful to the Sonoma, California Public Library and the St. Helena Wine Library, St. Helena, California for making available many of the above books and for the interest and cooperation of their staffs.

A. J. G.